THE MANAGER'S POCKET GUIDE TO

Employee Relations

by
Terry L. Fitzwater

HRD PRESS
Amherst, Massachusetts

Published by:

HRD Press
22 Amherst Road
Amherst, MA 01002
1-800-822-2801 (U.S. and Canada)
413-253-3488
413-253-3490 (fax)
www.hrdpress.com

ISBN 0-87425-476-0

Cover design by Eileen Klockars
Editorial services by Mary George
Production services by CompuDesign

Printed in Canada

FOREWORD

Terry Fitzwater has once again written a concise and extremely useful guide for human resources managers—this time focusing on providing managers with the tools necessary to motivate employees and to resolve disputes in the workplace before they become serious legal issues. Terry's approach is straightforward, easy to apply, and geared to today's changing workforce. It is a welcome contribution to the literature on this topical subject.

John M. Skonberg
Attorney
Littler Mendelson

TABLE OF CONTENTS

Preface

Management. I once heard it referred to as a "series of healthy disagreements." It's not a bad definition, if you think about it. A company's employees will not always agree on how to resolve the problems and challenges that are a part of every business day.

> **MANAGEMENT IS A SERIES OF HEALTHY DISAGREEMENTS.**

Resolution is always the goal, and it's what's expected of a person in a leadership position. Decision making with the wise use of resources is what moves a company.

There are a number of facets and skills required to perform in any position of authority, and all of them must be learned if you are to be an effective leader. They include skills in communications, delegation, performance review, and discipline, as well as skills and knowledge associated with the use and application of the company's policies and procedures. One skill is becoming even more important: a thorough understanding of all the employment laws that impact a business. Each one affects the manager's relationship with his or her employees, a relationship that, because of downsizing and the resultant need to work "leaner and meaner," is more vulnerable than ever before.

What is interesting about this is the fact that very few people in leadership positions are initially trained to handle **all** of the aspects of being a manager. Many were elevated to their current positions because of a recognized technical skill and, after all, who better to promote than those individuals? The story goes something like this: "Jane your work is excellent. It has been so for quite some time. To acknowledge your contributions, we are promoting you to a management position." This is all well and good (good performance should be rewarded), but an important step is sometimes missed: training. Training managers to become managers is critical to the success of the company as well as to the individual manager.

It is not at all unusual to use "180-degree feedback" when discussing a manager's performance. It's also not unusual to learn that some new managers are not performing to employee expectation. I've seen many a feedback statement highlight the lack of training on the part of the manager. It is likely to show up on attitude surveys, as well. If you believe what you read, feedback these days seems to focus on the manager's lack of personal involvement with the employee. This is not necessarily negative: In fact, it's good when comments center on the need for attention and not on some other deficiency.

Can something be done to fix this situation? Absolutely. That "something" is what this book is all about. The idea came from my firsthand experience as a human resources executive. Too often my company had to promote people before they were ready due to shortages of talent. To address this problem I developed a training program called "Working with People." The idea was to make sure that managers were provided with the tools they needed in order to manage. The most important tools are those that offer ways to increase interactions between management and employees. If that relationship is sound, then everything else will fall into place.

> ## A MANAGEMENT NECESSITY: MANAGING RELATIONSHIPS.

Historical Perspective

The dominant management style of the 1960's was **reactive**. It is now **proactive** and **integrated**.

Years	Skills	Style
1960's–1970's **Reactive**	Controllers Compliance	Hire and Fire
1970's–1980's **Proactive**	Benchmarkers Functional Experts	
1990's–? **Integrated**	Change Agents Organizationally Astute	Teams to the Task

Management skills changed to keep up with the changing work environment and new philosophies. It was no longer acceptable to be a technician versed in controlling and compliance. It became a necessity, beginning in the early 1990's, to have an in-depth understanding of the needs of the organization and its people. Motivation by fear was replaced with motivation by participation.

This book covers issues in relationship management and an overview of employment laws that impact that relationship. It will offer several ideas toward developing a more satisfied workforce and a company more informed about some common employment laws.

The Purpose of this Guide
The intent of this guide is:

- To give those new to the process of management (or anyone needing a few new ideas and tools concerning relationship management) some insight into the key skills needed to be successful.

- To provide audit and survey materials to help managers evaluate and assess skills and policies to gain an understanding of "holes" where change may be necessary.

- To provide a number of suggestions on programs and philosophies in order to increase an employee's satisfaction and desire to stay with an organization.

INTRODUCTION

Before a company or its management executes its employee relations strategy, it must first set the expectation for change. That is, it must demonstrate through its actions that change and the employee's agreement or disagreement are acceptable.

PREPARE—PROVIDE—PARTICIPATE—PRACTICE

Prepare the group for change. Actively solicit feedback to set the stage for interactive, unfiltered, information exchange.

Provide support for this new philosophy of risk taking. Demonstrate through your actions that acts of co-mission are always preferred to acts of omission.

Participate with the group. Management by walking around is better than desktop management.

Practice the arts of communication, delegation, and empowerment. Trust the group to respond positively to your supportive management style.

EMPLOYEE RELATIONS TOP TEN VOCABULARY	
Empower	Delegation
Trust	Participation
Input	Motivation
Communication	Direction/Guidance
Feedback	Coach

With this as our background, let's begin with a look at material designed to increase management and employee interaction, keeping in mind these top-ten words about employee relations.

Employee Relations Audit

Why audit our employee relations practices? To establish a baseline from which we can make educated corrective decisions.

> **SYSTEMS MUST CHANGE WHEN VALUES CHANGE.**

Another way of describing the shift from yesterday's work values to those of today may be more familiar: *"I do not live to work, I work to live."*

Let's look at how worker values have changed.

TRADITIONAL *vs.* NEW VALUES

❏ Live for the future	Live for today
❏ Leisure activities are not a priority	Time away from the job is important
❏ Hard work is its own reward	My family is my reward
❏ A job may infringe on my personal time	A job should seldom infringe on my time
❏ I need occasional feedback and recognition	On the job recognition should be frequent
❏ I don't care if work is boring	Work must be satisfying, rewarding, and challenging
❏ Money is my security for what it buys	Money is used to experience life now

To the manager, this values shift translates into paying attention to the little things in order to keep them from becoming insurmountable problems, and developing systems and programs where necessary because a manager's time is so limited. Our goal then *is* satisfaction.

The message is this: Employee perceptions are determined by management practices and styles and whether they are controlling or empowering, and the organization's policies and procedures and whether these are strictly interpreted or directional in nature. If we take this model and create the best

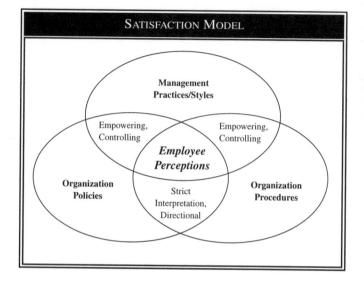

working environment for all employees, we would then have
empowered employees who use policies and procedures that
are directional in nature.

> ## STRICT INTERPRETATION OF
> ## POLICIES AND PROCEDURES
> ## LIMITS EMPLOYEE CREATIVITY.

If an organization is to have good, interactive relationships
between management and staff, it must have at a minimum
an open door policy; a complaint procedure; progressive discipline; a two-way communications network/system; and a

performance review system with major employee input. Here's a quick way to determine how your employees view these "musts." Distribute this matrix at a staff meeting and ask employees to rate each item.

How Would You Rate the Following?			
	Very Good	Average	Poor
Open Door Policy			
Complaint Procedure			
Progressive Discipline			
Communications			
Performance Review Process			

Request that each person check off a response and write a brief statement next to it that indicates his or her understanding of each process. Let's define each for our own understanding.

Open Door Policy—A system that allows an individual to see any person, at any time, for any reason. This system fails most of the time because of management. For example, if an employee comes to a manager and the manager says he or she is "unavailable—come back and see me tomorrow," would the employee consider the company to have an open door policy? I can tell you from experience he or she would not. (A sample policy is included in Appendix I.)

Complaint Procedure—A system that allows an individual to be heard and to voice his or her opinion on treatment, procedures, work hours, and other issues of work concern. No subject is taboo if the system is to work. A sound procedure will include time frames for response. A "no" response to an employee's question *is* a response. It may not be the one the person wants to hear, but it is **action**.

Progressive Discipline—A system of action steps that precede termination, except in the most serious cases. The steps normally consist of verbal, written, and final discussions before discharge. (A progressive discipline system is included in the book *Documenting Employee Performance,* published by HRD Press, 1998.)

Communications—A good communications network/system can make or break the company because it relates to employee satisfaction. Misinformation in the wrong hands is ammunition for dissent. In order for communications to be effective, remember this word: **FATE**. It is an acronym for frequent, accurate, timely, and educational.

REMEMBER ➤ Frequent—Accurate—Timely— Educational

There is another word that comes to mind for the letter T: Trusted. Remember that communications does not simply happen. It is strategically planned.

> ## COMMUNICATIONS IS A PLANNED ACTIVITY.

Communication and information sharing are integral parts of every staff, departmental, or divisional meeting. No subject is taboo. I know of one company that shuts down its operation once every three months from 11:30 A.M. to 1:30 P.M. to meet with all of its employees. There is not one topic closed to discussion. Information is presented on plan achievement, expansion possibilities, new opportunities for product development, etc. At the end of the meeting, a microphone is passed around for questions or responses to what has been shared. How do the employees feel about this? Trusted . . . Included . . . A part of an organization that has no hidden agendas.

> ## INFORMED PEOPLE MAKE INFORMED DECISIONS.

I don't want communications to sound too easy. Good communications takes practice and time to build to a point of organizational comfort. (We will look at communications in more detail in Chapter 1.)

Performance Review Process—There is nothing quite as demotivating as a one-sided performance discussion. This process, much like communication, must have joint participation if it is to be effective. The review will basically contain three parts: what is good about the performance; what needs improvement; and a **mutually agreeable** action plan on how to improve performance. Remember: Employee input leads to a feeling of ownership and a desire to correct a deficiency.

Let's shift gears a bit. Here is a matrix concerning organization **musts** regarding intent vs. policy.

How Would You Rate the Following?			
	Very Good	Average	Poor
Job security			
Benefits			
Wages			
Working conditions			
Fair policies/procedures			
Workload/pressure			

Our goal, just as before, is to find out what the employees think concerning the organization. Take the answers and develop a response matrix to isolate problematic areas. For example,

Issue	EMPLOYEE Comments
Job security	Constant change, Downsizing
Wages	Below local community average
Workload/pressure	Too demanding because of downsizing

Your action plan will look like this:

Issue	EMPLOYEE Comments

Wages: Perceived as below local community average.

To Do:

1. Identify others in our same line of business.
2. Conduct a wage/salary survey.
3. Compare average wages to our own.
4. Consider adjustments if necessary.
5. Share information with the employees.

The goal of each matrix is employee satisfaction gained through participation in problem solving.

OWNERSHIP BEGINS WITH PARTICIPATION.

It is important to emphasize the need to follow up if you decide to ask for employee input. Nothing is more frustrating than to give an opinion and then be kept in the dark about how it is perceived or what will become of it.

Communications

Communications. Effective management starts here. The ability to understand and to be understood cannot be overemphasized and it is not easy. It is also an imperative to sound employee relations. It will drive every activity and correctly direct and guide, or unfortunately misinform. What we must avoid, as was said to Paul Newman in *Cool Hand Luke*, is this statement: "What we have here is a failure to communicate."

> ### MISCOMMUNICATION IS AT THE ROOT OF ALL DISAGREEMENTS.

Linguists state that the English language does not do us any favors. Take the word *fast*. It has multiple meanings such as: someone is fleet of foot; has decided not to eat for a period of time; or is painting with a color guaranteed not to run. Compounding this problem are theories that most people retain 10% of what they hear and a typical person only hears one out of every four words stated to him or her. Here is another thought to ponder: The typical person, with the advent of e-mail and telephone mail, will have the opportunity to communicate well over 200 times a day. So, think about this: If you are totally understood 95% of the

1

time, you will still be misunderstood ten times. Ten times! The bottom line is, if you think you are understood each and every time you express yourself, you could be in for a big surprise.

The Phases of Communications

There are two parts to the process of communications: Someone speaking and someone listening. Both must be *in sync* for understanding to occur. Let's look at the table below.

THE WORDS	THE MUSIC
What I said	What was heard
What I displayed	What was seen
What I need	What the person wants

If the results listed above are the starting points of most conversations, how do we reconcile such a vast difference in agendas? Consider a five-step process to improve communications.

1. Analyze	• Listen for content
	• Determine the issue(s)
2. Synthesize	• Paraphrase to establish a mutually understood vocabulary
3. Sympathize	• Establish trust to build understanding
4. Energize	• Brainstorm action items and plans
5. Finalize	• Formalize responsibilities

Let's look at each step separately.

Analyze—This phase begins with *active* listening. Active listening requires focusing on the speaker and the full content of the message rather than a response; eliminating environmental distractions such as telephone calls, noise from the hallway, or people "popping" in and out of the office during a conversation; and prejudging the message based on the content or the speaker.

Synthesize—This is the *clarify* phase. The easiest method to use to increase understanding in a conversation is to paraphrase. Remember the following phrase and use it whenever you are not clear you understood a speaker: *"If I heard you correctly, here is what you said."* Repetition will clear any misunderstandings of content and establish a vocabulary understood by both parties.

Sympathize—This phase is sometimes lost in the heat of discussion or in the confusion of the moment. Do not let that happen. Sympathy will build trust, and trust leads to open and frank communications. The bottom line is that a person is more apt to share information, even sensitive feedback or constructive criticism, to a trusted co-communicator: a person who knows it's not personal, it's business.

Energize—This phase turns discussion into actions and into actionable plans. The key is to get the plans down on paper with language understood by both parties. Nothing should be committed to paper until there is mutual agreement on content and meaning.

Finalize—If the first four steps are successful this is an easy phase to implement. It is nothing more than establishing (1) who has the responsibility (2) to do what (3) by what date. Plans will thus look as follows:

Action Items:	Who:	Due Date:
Complete sales budgets for IS department	John Smith	By September 15

Team Communications

Most organizations today assemble and disassemble teams to address problems or issues on an as-needed basis. This will add to the difficulty of effective communications, as those unfamiliar with the group's or department's culture, norms, and technologies join in to problem-solve. When teams assemble or individuals need to look at roles and responsibilities, remember the flow chart on the next page.

The chart may look busy, but it is quite simple to understand and to put into action by assigning phases to the process.

Phase I
This phase begins with the *issue* and its *impact on others*. If the issue is limited, there is little impact on others, and problem resolution is accomplished by defining and refining the issue until action planning leads to problem resolution.

Phase II
If the problem affects others, you will need to identify all the *stakeholders* who will form the *appropriate team members*. This is an important step in establishing ownership;

Process for Effective Communications

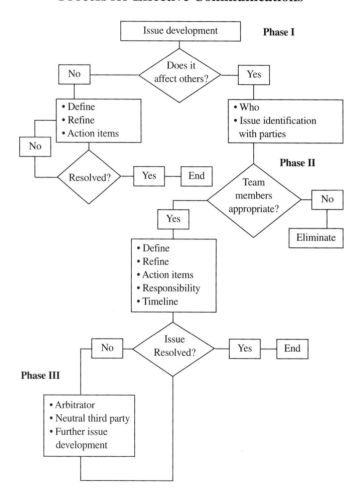

INCLUSION CREATES OWNERSHIP .

no individual likes to be left out of a problem when he or she feels able to contribute or believes it is a part of his or her knowledge base or "territory."

ALWAYS SEARCH EXHAUSTIVELY FOR THE STAKEHOLDERS.

This team will be charged with the responsibility to define and refine the issues and action items, assigning responsibilities and timelines for task completion or "report outs" to the group for consensus decision making.

Phase III
This marks the completion of the task. It also gives the group an opportunity to bring in others if there is some kind of bottleneck or decision disagreement. A neutral third party, such as the director or vice president of the function, will hear or look at the issue and assist the group in decision making.

Now that we understand the importance of communications, let's move to a proven methodology for sounding out employee feelings and perceptions with the use of survey instruments.

Satisfaction Surveys

Team survey instruments allow you to do two things:
(1) examine the skills of the management team, and (2)
measure the satisfaction of employee teams. If you
concentrate on addressing one problem without the other,
you may be dooming yourself to failure. No amount of supervisory skill can overcome a group's inner dissatisfaction with
itself, and no amount of group harmony will overcome a
manager not in tune with his or her group.

The survey process itself consists of five phases. Each phase
will add clarification and provide direction to management and
employees regarding the ultimate goal of issue resolution.

Here is something **important** to remember: *Anytime you ask
an employee for his or her input, you set the expectation for
some kind of action or answer.* The fact that you are
including them in data review meetings and action planning
sends a strong signal that their input matters. You can
increase the impact of that message by appointing various
employee teams or task forces to work on implementing any
suggestions. Let's look at two survey instruments that you
can tailor to your specific needs: The Manager Communications Survey and the Work Group Communications Survey.

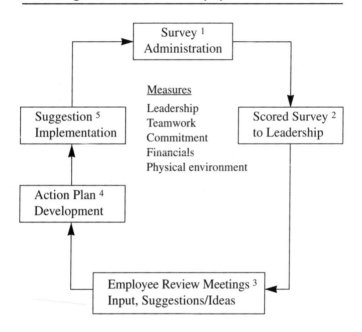

The Manager Communications Survey

No employee relations review is complete without evaluating the performance of the manager **from the perspective** of the employee. This can be intimidating. It requires trust and an ability to understand that feedback is not meant to be personal, but is instead another avenue for growth. A process known as 180-degree feedback can be very useful. If handled properly it will open channels of communication; build, establish, and maintain relationships of mutual trust; lead to team building; and break down barriers. Let's look at a survey designed to measure factors ranging from giving and receiving feedback to leadership.

Manager Communications Survey

My Manager	Agree		Neutral			Disagree	
	1	2	3	4	5	6	7
1. Is available when needed							
2. Makes me feel comfortable							
3. Often solicits my input and ideas							
4. Is commited to my development							
5. Looks after my best interests							
6. Can be counted on for information							
7. Does timely performance reviews							
8. Is receptive to feedback							
9. Meets with me regularly							
10. Meets with our group regularly							
11. Expands my knowledge with developmental assignments							
12. Encourages group interaction and problem solving							
13. Communicates frequently							
14. Establishes clear, objective goals							
15. Has thoroughly explained my job to me							
16. Is receptive to new ideas to streamline work							
17. Provides tools to do the job							
18. Listens and responds to my concerns							
19. Lets me know when I have done a good job							
20. Empowers me to do my job							
21. Is fair and inspires confidence							

This kind of survey will provide information to the manager on the employee's perception of managerial support. More importantly, managerial **credibility** will be greatly enhanced if the departmental manager distributes the survey to the employees and asks for their input. A pre-survey statement might say:

"I have asked you here today to participate in a survey. The survey will assist me in identifying the tools this group needs to work more efficiently. It will also ask a number of questions designed to help me work on the skills I need to work more effectively with each of you. The survey is completely anonymous, so please feel free to answer honestly."

Scoring the survey

To score the survey, look at the responses to each question, add the numbers together, and then divide that total by the number of participants. Let's look at an example. You give the survey to six people. On question number 1, the group checks the following numbers, 3, 5, 5, 6, 4, and 7. If you add these numbers together, the sum is 30. Now, divide your answer by the number of employees taking the survey (6). The average response (30 divided by 6) is 5. Each question is scored the same way. This will provide the information you need to graph the responses.

Once you graph the responses (see the sample graph on page 11), you will be able to isolate the most problematic areas: any response in the range of five and up is worth discussing. In this case, question numbers 5, 6, 11, 12, 15, and 20 appear to be problem issues. You must develop an action plan to

Sample graph.

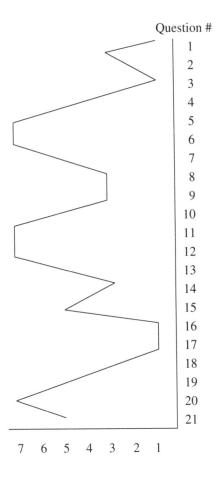

correct each one. For instance, let's assume employees rate question 3, "Often solicits my input and ideas" as needing attention. A supervisor's action plan might be:

ACTION ITEMS

1. Ask for plan input at staff meetings.

2. Establish a departmental suggestion box.

3. Walk through the department several times each week in order to be more available for ideas and questions.

4. Conduct bi-weekly meetings to solicit employee input.

Be creative and include your employees. They will have suggestions for you.

Let's look at another example.

Question 19: "My manager lets me know when I've done a good job."

ACTION ITEMS

1. Look for every opportunity to compliment instead of criticize.

2. Create an awards program to recognize individual and team achievements.

3. Establish a monthly (pizza) party to reward employees for departmental achievements.

As the examples demonstrate, your action plans do not need to be monumental. You are not looking for revolutionary action; you are looking for *evolutionary action*. Remember that subtle changes over time can completely change your style, employee perception, group achievement, and overall culture.

Tailoring the survey

The strength of these kinds of surveys is that they can be tailored to fit any situation when you want to solicit feedback on any issue. As an example, let's assume that a manager wants to know if he or she praises *as well as* criticizes. Two questions could be added:

My Manager:

1. Provides well-deserved praise

and:

2. Is sometimes quick to criticize without all of the facts

Tailoring the survey requires nothing more than a little thinking about how to ask the right questions to guide, direct, and resolve problem issues.

Another way to add value to the survey is to add a comments section at the end of the survey form. For example,

Are there any other comments that you would like to share that were not covered by the survey questions?

_____

_____

The Work Group Communications Survey

There are times when a manager needs to closely examine his or her team in order to identify intact work group issues. The Work Group Communications Survey is a tool designed to surface inter/intra group issues relating to communications; mechanisms for mutual support; roles and responsibilities; and the ability of a group to work efficiently with others.

Work Group Communications Survey

			Agree		Neutral			Disagree

Our Team	1	2	3	4	5	6	7
1. Has easily understood goals and objectives							
2. Expects results to be rewarded							
3. Is challenged by what we are asked to do							
4. Is a cohesive unit							
5. Supports one another							
6. Is viewed as a business partner by other units							
7. Is effective in exchanging ideas and information							
8. Encourages its members to take risks.							
9. Knows its roles and responsibilities							
10. Has the autonomy to get the job done							
11. Meets frequently							

Our Team	1	2	3	4	5	6	7
12. Has needed resources available							
13. Encourages member productivity							
14. Has a high level of member trust							
15. Has the need for change explained to us							
16. Communicates clearly							
17. Members are not reluctant to give constructive feedback to each other							
18. Works efficiently without a designated leader							
19. Is trained to accomplish its mission							
20. Knows how to resolve internal conflicts							
21. Has a clearly understood mission statement							

Chart the responses as for the Manager Communications Survey. The manager will show the work group the responses and charge them with the responsibility to develop an action plan to resolve the issues. Giving them an example of a plan will help set them on a correct course. Let's look at an example you can use with the group.

Our team:

"Is effective in exchanging ideas and information."

ACTION PLAN
1. Meet at the beginning of the shift to discuss the day's activities.
2. Appoint a team member to act as a liaison with our manager to make sure information flows to the team.
3. Establish quarterly team meetings to discuss accomplishments *vs.* plan.

This is a team-building exercise; it not only builds trust among the members, it breaks down barriers between the group and the manager. The flow of information will thus increase and the trust the group has in itself will grow.

Alternative Dispute Resolution

Audits and surveys set the framework for solid employee relations practices because they help the organization focus on areas that need attention or that might become problematic. We will now turn our attention to dispute resolution because no matter how hard we try, there will always be some level of disagreement. The methodology used should complement the organization's style and bring about swift resolution.

Most companies have some type of complaint procedure. However, because some level of management has the final say in deciding the outcome, it may be viewed as a biased procedure. Three methods are available that can reduce or eliminate that perception.

TYPE OF COMPLAINT PROCEDURE	DECISION MAKER
Advisory Arbitration	External
Ombudsman	Internal
Employee Decisional Review (EDR)	Internal

All three methods channel decision making to parties **outside** the normal chain of command. Advisory arbitration grants it to a third party not affiliated with the company, and in the EDR and ombudsman programs, decision making is kept internal but still outside a normal chain of command.

As you review these programs, keep in mind that an organization can make its complaint procedure as broad or as narrow in scope as it chooses. The company will decide if challenges are encouraged on any issue or, as is the case in collective bargaining, limit them to wages, hours, and working conditions. I suggest you limit complaints to wages, hours, and working conditions so you do not get inappropriate challenges pertaining to issues such as proprietary strategic planning.

External Review
Advisory Arbitration

Let's first make a distinction between *advisory* arbitration and the more common *binding* arbitration. In advisory arbitration, the arbitrator will state his or her findings: "It appears to me that there is a finding of fault and here is what I **recommend**." In binding arbitration, the arbitrator will state: "It appears there is a finding of fault and here is what you **will do**." As you can see, the difference is significant. In advisory arbitration, the company is not obligated to comply *but usually does* if the arbiter's decision and reasoning is sound. To do otherwise would make a sham of the process, and your employees would probably view it as such. In this guide I will discuss only advisory arbitration because it is generally less controversal with the workforce.

The American Arbitration Association (AAA) is one organization providing advisory arbitration. This association is comprised of arbitrators who are judges, lawyers, and educators; all are experts in the field of employment law and skilled at reviewing and making decisions on rules, contracts, and/or laws as to whether the rule, etc., was interpreted and applied as it was intended. For example, if you have a policy stating that an employee is subject to termination for excessive absenteeism and you take such action, based on the policy the arbiter will:

1. Look at policy language to determine if you have defined "excessive" (e.g., five times in one month) and will review and rule on such questions on a case by case basis.

2. Look at past practice to see if you have been consistent in the application of the rule. It helps determine if the employee was on notice as to what the policy meant.

3. Determine if there were extenuating circumstances for the absenteeism that were not taken into consideration or given due consideration.

Serious cases

Normally, the use of advisory arbitration is limited to issues of "extreme importance or seriousness" (termination) because there is a fee for the services of the arbitrator. The employee should pay a portion of the fee to discourage capricious use of arbitration. A rate of one-half the cost of arbitration is recommended, with the company paying the other half. If the fee is $600, for example, the company will pay $300 and the employee will pay $300 to get the case to arbitration. This 50% arrangement creates a sense of ownership and makes the employee think, before bringing the action, about the relative merits of the need for third-party review. However, if the arbitrator finds the company at fault, the company should consider reimbursing the employee for his or her share. It's a good employee relations move.

Internal Review
Ombudsman

Webster's New World Dictionary defines ombudsman as "*public officials appointed to investigate citizens' complaints that may be infringing on the rights of individuals*." For our purpose, let's change it just a little: "Company officials appointed to investigate employee complaints."

The "official" can be either a management or a nonmanagement employee. The requirements for the appointee are that he or she have an understanding of the company's policies, procedures, employee handbooks, and other directional materials. The appointed individual conducts his or herself as an arbitrator who must sort fact from fiction and understand the company's past practice (precedent).

To be effective, the position of ombudsman should be a full-time position for a specified period of time. A one-year period will provide the ombudsman with enough experience to render knowledgeable decisions. The person must also operate outside the normal chain of command and be responsible to no one individual. It is critical that the person is perceived as **totally** impartial.

Employee Decisional Review

The EDR is made up of a group of employees appointed to review the decisions of management. This formal process is usually put into practice when a terminated employee challenges the action by presenting his or her case to the EDR board. To resolve an issue like this management grants authority and defines the scope of the EDR, usually limiting it to issues involving wages, hours, and working conditions.

EDR membership

Members of the EDR board, like the ombudsman, are appointed for a specified period of time. Each member should represent a different function and a different job category. The following information comes from a company that uses the EDR process:

Function	Classification
Accounting	Exempt Manager
Distribution	Hourly
R&D	Nonexempt
Engineering	Exempt Nonmanagement
Office and Clerical	Nonexempt
Warehousing	Hourly

Notice the makeup of the group. There are two hourly, two exempt, and two nonexempt employees; one of the exempts holds a management position. Most departments are represented, from accounting to warehousing. I highly recommend using such a diverse cross section format. The rationale is simple: Every employee will see that this committee is unbiased in composition. Any decision upheld or overturned by such an EDR group will not be subject to second-guessing *because of its composition*.

Retention through Satisfaction

Downsizing. Rightsizing. Layoffs. Reengineering. The 1990s have added a few new words to the vocabulary of the American workforce. Here are a few more. *Discontent. Dissatisfaction. Malaise.* These words have led many to ask the question, "Whatever happened to worker loyalty?" The answer: It left with the first wave of cost-cutting done at the expense of employees. Let's face it, it is difficult to maintain any sense of loyalty when one is waiting for the next shoe to drop.

The cure: Treat the problem as another management issue that must be resolved. Here is a quick and simple process to help reassure your employees.

> - **IDENTIFY THE ISSUE.**
> - **INVOLVE THE EMPLOYEES.**
> - **IMPLEMENT THE IDEAS.**

Identify the Issue

The issue defined in this book is *satisfaction*. Yours and your employees'. However, there is a side issue plaguing business, and that is **retention**. Retention is getting a lot of attention in the mainstream press. Employee turnover is costly and it must be controlled. The key is to restore a sense of security and self-worth in your staff; then you **will** control turnover.

Involve the Employees

Empowerment is a way to immediately increase the level of satisfaction in your organization and this has been the case since the first practitioners of scientific management plied their trade over 50 years ago.

> ## EMPOWERMENT CREATES OWNERSHIP.

The message is clear to anyone who wants to resolve any type of employee-related issue: The employee *cares about issues in which he or she has a vested interest.*

Implement the Ideas

Vested interest leads to employee satisfaction because of the ownership it creates. Ultimately, employee-generated issue resolution leads to retention.

There are a number of areas where management can affect satisfaction.

AREAS OF IMPACT	
Management Practices	Personal Development
Empowerment	Recognition
Communications	Family
Management Philosophies	Job-Related Training

Much of what you are about to read was gathered from a benchmarking effort that took place over a five-year period. The ideas presented worked for others and they will work for you, but only if you invest the time, **with your employees**, in discussing whether or not a particular program or philosophy is right for your organization. I promise you this: The mere fact that you are discussing the subject of satisfaction will raise the present levels of satisfaction *immediately*. The bottom line is that if you are looking for a culture change or searching for additional ways to re-instill loyalty, don't hesitate to begin! Don't hesitate to demonstrate to each employee that *yours* is the organization of choice. To paraphrase Betty Davis, "Fasten your seat belts. This is going to be some kind of ride."

The "Messages to Management" included in this Pocket Guide are short statements designed to make you think and react to the statement with some kind of plan. Each message is followed by a list of practical ways you can increase employee loyalty, decrease retention, and address employee relations issues. The more actions you implement, the greater your chances of making a positive impact on your staff. For example,

> "For every message that flows down the chain of command. . .
>
> . . . a mechanism should exist to ensure that another message goes back up."

> ## ENHANCE COMMUNICATIONS.

A "To Do" from this statement:

Ask yourself if you or your company makes it easy for an employee to voice an opinion. If not, why not? And what will you do about it?

Some of the messages that follow are subtle, some are not. I think you will find them fun, if nothing else. But try to go with the flow and see if you can think of any actionable items yourself.

MESSAGES TO MANAGEMENT

❑ Poor performance has one of two root causes . . .
  . . . a deficiency in comprehension or a deficiency in execution.

❑ If something feels right at the top of the organization . . .
  . . . you may want to rethink it.

❑ If we practice the golden rule at work . . .
  . . . why are there so many work rules?

❑ If you have an open door policy . . .
  . . . why do so many of your offices have doors?

Management Philosophies

Management sets the stage for change in this phase. It has been said that actions speak louder than words. It's time to speak.

TOLERATE MISTAKES	If you want to increase risk taking, avoid punishing or taking issue with the *occasional* mistake. You will find that acts of *co-mission* will soon replace acts of omission.

ELIMINATE OFFICES	Send a strong message of "all for one and one for all." This practice is really catching on: offices exist *only* for confidential meetings, performance reviews, customer meetings, etc.

ELIMINATE DOORS	There is nothing as liberating as knowing you have the freedom to go wherever you need to, and see whomever you want at any time you

wish. It encourages problem solving and the free flow of information.

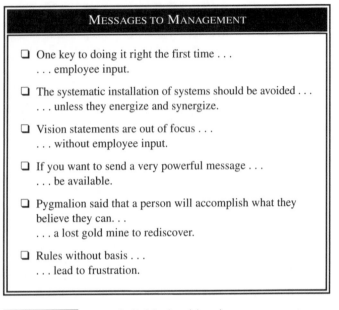

MESSAGES TO MANAGEMENT

❏ One key to doing it right the first time . . .
   . . . employee input.

❏ The systematic installation of systems should be avoided . . .
   . . . unless they energize and synergize.

❏ Vision statements are out of focus . . .
   . . . without employee input.

❏ If you want to send a very powerful message . . .
   . . . be available.

❏ Pygmalion said that a person will accomplish what they
   believe they can. . .
   . . . a lost gold mine to rediscover.

❏ Rules without basis . . .
   . . . lead to frustration.

TREAT EMPLOYEES . . . as individuals with unique problems, concerns, issues, and needs. Meet often in their territory, not in your office.

TREAT EMPLOYEES . . . as equals. The "we/they" mentality should be replaced with "us."

TREAT EMPLOYEES . . . as business partners capable of understanding the needs of the business. Don't think employees won't understand the financials or other aspects of the business. They will if you take the time to teach them.

LET PYGMALION

. . . become your primary belief. If you tell employees they are capable of doing and learning, they are likely to produce the desired result. We are all capable of becoming or achieving what we think we can.

MESSAGES TO MANAGEMENT

❑ Loyalty lost is like a field of dreams . . .
   . . . rebuild it and they will come.

❑ Take charge and set your own agenda . . .
   . . . before someone does it for you.

❑ Interested in what's going on in the fiefdom?
   Get out of the castle.

❑ Recurrent downsizing helps the bottom line in two ways . . .
   . . . it eliminates the chosen and it eliminates those
   unwilling to wait for the next shoe to drop.

❑ Standard operating procedures . . .
   . . . put limits on employee creativity.

❑ To inspire ownership . . .
   . . . treat your employees as they really are: partners.

ONLY TERMINATE

. . . as a last resort and after several employee/manager interactive coaching sessions, and only after you follow a discipline procedure.

LEAD BY EXAMPLE	Eliminate the "do as I say, not as I do" mentality. Lend a hand, even if the opportunity does not present itself. Availability is your new watchword.
ONLY DOWNSIZE	. . . as a last resort. If a budget can be cut instead of an employee, do it.

Management Practices

Good management practices humanize the manager.

MANAGEMENT BY WALKING AROUND	Get out of the office and take a note pad with you. You never know when you will be asked a question you will need to research. Write down a name and respond quickly.

MESSAGES TO MANAGEMENT

❑ Change is more easily accomplished . . .
 . . . when employees champion the change.

❑ If employees aren't motivated by anyone in the chain of command . . .
 . . . look first to the chain's main link.

❑ If you say you will do something about it . . .
 . . . do something about it.

❑ Absolute power . . .
 . . . disrupts absolutely.

❑ Management's prerogative . . .
 . . . is an oxymoron.

❑ Bored of directors . . .
 . . . is spelled correctly.

VISIT THE OFF SHIFTS	You can make points quickly by making an appearance on shifts you normally don't visit. Make sure you hit the break areas. Take notes.

AFFIRMATIVE ACTION, SAFETY, HEALTH, ENVIRONMENT, ANTI-VIOLENCE	Be the employer of choice through your efforts to create a workforce with true concern for all. Publish your policies and any community actions you take.

COMPLAINT PROCEDURE, OMBUDSMAN, EDR	Quick resolution keeps small problems from becoming larger company-wide issues. Nip everything in the bud and as quickly as possible. Any response to an issue that takes more than 72 hours is too slow.

MESSAGES TO MANAGEMENT

❑ Empowerment is only effective . . .
  . . . when you willingly turn power loose.
❑ Ever-increasing spans of power control . . .
  . . . unleash potential exponentially.
❑ Doubts are nothing more than speed bumps . . .
  . . . on the road to discovery.
❑ Strike gold through training and development . . .
  . . . mine your own business.
❑ Discover an employee's niche . . .
  . . . to uncover and unleash talents.
❑ Elevating goals will not elevate . . .
  . . . unless they are perceived as obtainable.

Personal Development

Management philosophies and practices restore faith in the organization and provide the bedrock for change. A large part of retention now shifts to enhancing the perception that there is an opportunity for growth. The concept of **empowerment** flows through each of the following ideas, but keep in mind that empowerment consists of two parts: (1) the willingness to grant power, and (2) employee acceptance of it. It is not just enough to grant it, you must *train* employees to accept it.

ENCOURAGE LEARNING	Make it easy for everyone to enhance his or her skills, regardless of whether or not it is directly related to their job. Develop a

methodology. There is no reason why a shipping clerk cannot be an accounting clerk with the proper training or schooling.

MESSAGES TO MANAGEMENT

- ❏ Performance reviews are only as informative . . .
  . . . as the reviewer.
- ❏ If you think feedback is a term used exclusively in the music business . . .
  . . . you probably have communications issues.
- ❏ The only way to achieve mutual understanding . . .
  . . . is to make sure your dictionaries are published by the same company.
- ❏ If you only meet annually to discuss results with employees . . .
  . . . you've probably lost them for the remaining eleven months.

| **TUITION REFUND** | Pay a portion of the expenses so that employees can return to college or take part in other training seminars. A standard policy is 80% of tuition, fees, and books. |

| **360 FEEDBACK** | A process where bosses, peers, and subordinates provide performance-related feedback. The purpose is to increase employee |

awareness of how others view the employee's performance and to work on areas of skill deficiency.

| **180 FEEDBACK** | A process where subordinates provide performance-related feedback. The purpose is to build on interdepartmental relationships as they relate to perceptions of their manager. |

| **SABBATICAL** | A leave of absence, for a specified period of time, to pursue educational or professional learning experiences. |

MESSAGES TO MANAGEMENT

- ❏ The best predictor of future success . . .
  . . . past success and learning from mistakes.

- ❏ Effort coupled with praise . . .
  . . . a formula for *sustainable* performance.

- ❏ To increase the likelihood of something good reoccurring . . .
  . . . positively acknowledge the act.

- ❏ Mission statements are impossible missions . . .
  . . . without employee input.

- ❏ Policy manuals should be replaced with . . .
  . . . reward and recognition manuals.

- ❏ To increase satisfaction over time . . .
  . . . celebrate the little things every day.

IDENTIFY THE FAST TRACK

Develop a process (e.g., a yearly review of all employees) to identify those who are ready for increased responsibilities. Don't make them wait. Promote them as soon as you can or the competition will do it for you.

PEER REVIEW

A concept similar to 360° feedback, except that it is limited to the individual's peers.

Recognition

Recognition is an important part of retention. The hectic pace of business often makes it very easy to criticize and forget to praise.

HOLIDAY DINNERS, BANQUETS, LUNCHEONS, POT LUCK, EMPLOYEE OF WEEK, MONTH OR YEAR, SERVICE AWARDS, PIZZA DAYS

Recognition programs come in many shapes and sizes. The best thing about adopting one, however, is that it does not matter what you choose. As the saying goes, *Just Do It.* Most of them involve very little expenditure, and if recognition is made in the presence of others it will add immeasurably to job satisfaction. Recognition doesn't necessarily mean rewards or awards. It can also be allowing a good performer to coach others, or making presentations to the senior leadership of the company. Try a PRIDE award— Personal Recognition for Individual Dedication to Excellence. Another idea is to invite the family to attend the presentation of the award.

MESSAGES TO MANAGEMENT

❏ Actions may speak louder than words . . .
 . . . but misguided words can cripple.

❏ Place people first . . .
 . . . or settle for second-best.

❏ To increase the likelihood of success and the longevity of any program . . .
 . . . instill a sense of ownership.

❏ Negativism is like a plague . . .
 . . . it spreads easily with little contact.

❏ Paradigm revisited . . .
 . . . employees as a competitive advantage.

❏ When you design your next critical path . . .
 . . . let it lead to your door.

MESSAGES TO MANAGEMENT

❏ If you want to know what is going on, answer your own telephone . . .
 . . . for every call you wish you hadn't taken, there will be ten others you'll be glad you did.

❏ For every employee who understands your message . . .
 . . . there will be ten others who do not.

❏ If we retain only 10% of what we hear . . .
 . . . why aren't we taking more notes?

❏ Your employee informational network is like your computer . . .
 . . . garbage in, garbage out.

Family Involvement

The role of the family in employee satisfaction and retention is often overlooked. Including the families of employees whenever possible makes them a part of the team and part of the work family.

> **FAMILY TO WORK DAYS, NEW HIRE ORIENTATION, FLOWERS TO SPOUSES OF NEW HIRES, ON-SITE DAY CARE, CONTRIBUTORY CHILD CARE, FLEX-TIME, JOB SHARING**

Invite the family to holiday get-togethers, recognition and service award banquets, and new hire orientation programs. Let each family member see and feel what the company is all about. Make it easy to come to work on time by providing on-site day care or flex-time. Job sharing is on the rise, where one person works from 8:00 A.M. to 12:00 P.M. and another from 1:00 P.M. to 5:00 P.M. Here's another good idea: If you reward an employee with a certificate for dinner, pay for the babysitting service. It's a nice touch that costs next to nothing. Another idea gaining in popularity is "Bring a child to work day." It's a good opportunity for them see what the parent is doing and why they leave home each day.

MESSAGES TO MANAGEMENT

❑ Task forces are more effective . . .
  . . . when members haven't been forced to the task.

❑ If you ask your organization to shoot for the stars . . .
  . . . that's as far as you can expect the rocket to fly.

❑ For maximum productivity . . .
  . . . plan your work and work your plan.

❑ A strong measure of your success as a manager . . .
  . . . the successful track record of those who report to you.

❑ Ability brings opportunity . . .
  . . . results sustain it.

❑ Focus groups are more effective . . .
  . . . when they help develop the focus.

Communications

Employees who are kept in the dark concerning the company and its plans are more apt to leave because *there is no clear reason to stay.* Always remember to ask yourself this question: "If we make this decision, who needs to know?" The answer is, *everyone.*

SUGGESTION
E-MAIL,
TELEPHONE
MESSAGING,
NEWSLETTERS,
MEETINGS,
OPINION
SURVEYS

The age of electronics provides a number of quick and easy ways to communicate. Part of its allure is that communication can be totally confidential, allowing those too timid to speak the opportunity to be heard. Meetings should be put on a regular schedule so that employees can prepare for them in advance. The employer's goal should be to create an open flow of information without encumbrances of any kind. Newsletters and similar in-house instruments are good ways to achieve this. They can also provide recognition if articles are written by employees on a rotating basis. Designating bulletin boards for employee use will enhance reader interest.

> ## MESSAGES TO MANAGEMENT
>
> ❑ Your raise becomes effective . . .
>   . . . when you are.
>
> ❑ To foster real continuous improvement . . .
>   . . . reward acts of co-mission to eliminate acts of omission.
>
> ❑ A formula for changing the ordinary to the extraordinary . . .
>   . . . empowerment coupled with trust.
>
> ❑ You will be judged in a moment . . .
>   . . . make sure it is the impression you want it to be.
>
> ❑ Consistency in any endeavor . . .
>   . . . diffuses confusion.

Performance Driven

Let performance and the ideas that spring from it provide another venue for employee satisfaction. These will take the form of *job-related training*.

PROMOTION FROM WITHIN, M.B.O.s, SUCCESS CRITERIA, CROSS TRAINING, JOB ROTATION

Never hire from the outside when a promotion is possible. Post a position's requirements and success criteria for all to see so your staff can assess their qualifications for the position. Make your list of positions available so if anyone desires to pursue another job, they will have an idea of what skills and performance standards they should adopt if they wish to advance.

Other

Here are a few more ideas to increase an employee's desire to remain with the company.

> **COLLEGE RECRUITING, PRESENTATIONS TO HIGH SCHOOLS AND CIVIC GROUPS, SHUTTLE BUSES, CONTRIBUTIONS OF TIME AND MONEY TO LOCAL CAUSES AND CHARITIES**

Any one of these ideas will get your name in front of the public and from a positive perspective. The idea is to have anyone seeking employment think of you first; your employees will feel a great deal of pride in telling others where they work. Bike-a-thons, walks for cancer, etc., coupled with the company's name emblazoned on a T-shirt, are a recruitment and retention gold mine at very little expense.

The manager or supervisor is the individual who ultimately influences satisfaction. Let's introduce an award for them. The **TEAM** award:

> ## TRAINING—EDUCATING—MENTORING

The award can be made to recognize the manager's efforts to develop each employee and help them to use their skills to their fullest potential. Remember, managers are people too. Recognizing their efforts increases satisfaction and keeps them around.

Do you remember our Employee Relations Top Ten Vocabulary? Let's revisit the list and add some definition. We'll call it the *words* and the *music*.

THE MANAGER'S TOP 10: THE WORDS

10 Words
I will provide daily **guidance and direction** to each employee.

9 Words
I will openly encourage employee **participation** in decision making.

8 Words
I will **delegate** for employee development and growth.

7 Words
I **trust** employees to do the job.

6 Words
I will continually **coach and counsel**.

5 Words
I will **lead** by example.

4 Words
Employee **input** is essential.

3 Words
Feedback is continual.

2 Words
Communicate daily.

1 Winning Word
Empower.

Here's how you do it.

THE MANAGER'S TOP 10: THE MUSIC	
Guidance and Direction	Mutually set goals, objectives, and completion dates.
Participation	Members of the team will problem solve together.
Delegation	Manage from a distance to allow for growth and learning.
Trust	Maintain an environment where fear of failure is minimized and failure is viewed as an opportunity for growth.
Coach and Counsel	Mentor to correct early deficiencies and acknowledge achievements.
Lead	Motivate by self-displayed standards and results.
Input	Messages are encouraged and acted upon.
Feedback	Measure and reward results continually.
Communicate	Minimize or eliminate barriers with open door/MBWA.
Empower	Move to a philosophy of trust to maximize potential.

The last two lists illustrate (and in fact define) today's management profile. The manager who utilizes the skills and talents of the work group and openly participates will reap the rewards of loyalty and, more importantly, achieve results through commitment.

Remember: *Effort, coupled with praise of results. . . . a formula for success.*

Let's now shift gears from employee relations to employment law. The next chapter provides an overview of the subject and includes a survey instrument to help you move toward compliance. This chapter is not intended to provide definitive explanations but rather to be a source to move you to action, especially if you are unfamiliar with the material.

Understanding Employment
Laws and Regulations

Do acronyms confuse you? Don't feel alone. Who wouldn't be frustrated trying to understand: FMLA, NLRB, WARN, EEOC, IRCA, ADEA, and BFOQ? To most people they are nothing more than a series of four-letter words. However, whether we like it or not, every manager must be conversant in their meaning. The reason is simple: Not knowing the meaning behind the letters can cost you. How? Well, let's say you decide to terminate a person's employment, and find after the fact that the person is part of a protected class (e.g., over the age of 40). While termination in and of itself is not against the law, it could be if the last ten people terminated were over 40. It begins to look as if someone is targeting a class or group that is legally protected from discrimination.

Let's test our knowledge before we discuss some of the more relevant laws.

MATCH THE LAW WITH ITS PREMISE
Directions: Draw a line to the correct definition

ADA	Either party can terminate at any time
ADEA	Mandates completion of I-9s
ERISA	Continues benefit coverage after termination
WARN	
BFOQ	Investigates charges of discrimination
COBRA	Prevents discrimination of the disabled
EEOC	Protection for those over 40
FLSA	Protects retirement entitlements
IRCA	Quid pro quo or hostile environment
Sexual Harassment	Requires a 60-day notice of layoffs or plant closings
FMLA	12 weeks to care for family issues
Employment at Will	Regulates overtime
	Male or female work assignments only
OSHA	Regulations to join or not join unions
NLRB	Regulations for a safe work environment
A.A.P.	
OFCCP	Agency that investigates progress where government contracts exist
	Details progress toward hiring, promotional goals, etc.

How do you think you did with the answers? Let's look at each definition and some of its sanctions, one at a time. We'll examine the ones that most frequently affect the management process. Keep in mind that this is not meant to be an all-encompassing review. Information on each of these regulations is available from government agencies listed in Appendix II.

ADA—AMERICANS WITH DISABILITIES ACT

This legislation was passed in 1990 to protect the rights of the disabled. Generally, it affects all employers with 15 or more employees. The definition of *disabled* includes people with mental retardation, or developmental disability (e.g., cerebral palsy); those who have a speech or hearing impairment; or people who are HIV positive, paralyzed, wheelchair-dependent, or who have partial or total blindness. Employers are required to (1) provide reasonable accommodation, (2) define the knowledge, skills, and abilities needed to perform the job, (3) train those who work with people with disabilities in how to more aptly assist and work with them, (4) revise health and medical examinations to avoid discrimination. Two of the above require further amplification.

"Reasonable Accommodation"

Reasonable accommodation is actively working to accommodate a disability. Examples include putting volume controls on telephones for the hearing impaired; altering facilities by putting bars in the restrooms or installing wheelchair ramps for accessibility; and allowing the use of flex-time to accommodate those who have medical or treatment appointments such as ongoing dialysis.

"Skills and Abilities"

This part of the act requires that employers document (usually through job descriptions) the essential functions of the job to make sure that there is no discrimination against a person with a disability. For example, if a position requires heavy lifting, the employer should not just write "heavy lifting." Specifics are needed, such as "unloading 150 lb. bags from the trucking dock and carrying them 10 feet to a conveyor system." Also remember that the employer must consider whether the employee can perform the essential functions through reasonable accomodation. The employer should also review the employment application and eliminate any questions relating to mental or physical impairment or disability. If there are exceptions, define them on the job description where specifications are required. A sample job description format that describes some ADA requirements is included in Appendix I.

Other Requirements of the ADA

Employee records are sometimes reviewed by others such as supervisors who are considering a person for promotion. To protect those who fall under the tenets of the ADA, all employee medical information must be confidential and maintained in a file separate from the employee's personnel file.

ADEA—AGE DISCRIMINATION IN EMPLOYMENT ACT OF 1967

This provision makes it illegal for employers with 20 or more employees to discriminate against those over the age of 40. The act originally covered those up to the age of 70, but was later amended and the age cap was eliminated. However, the age cap is applicable if there is a job-related occupational qualification. For example, the airline industry sets a mandatory retirement age of 60 for its pilots. While this is currently under debate, it is a recognized exclusion to this act.

When should an employer be concerned about this act? When the employer is making decisions that adversely affect employees over 40 but particularly when contemplating a reduction in its workforce. If a layoff is implemented and 9 of the 10 employees impacted (laid off) are covered by ADEA, the employer should look carefully at this need. While it may not be discrimination, for example, if the workforce is predominantly over 40, it certainly sends up a red flag. Never ignore the ADEA.

ERISA—EMPLOYEE'S RETIREMENT AND INCOME SECURITY ACT OF 1974

This law was enacted because of the potential for employer or union mismanagement of pension plans/funds. Employees who put money into company plans and expected plan payments at retirement were sometimes surprised to find that the money was not there. ERISA regulates pension plans and other benefit plans so that those who qualify for them can expect to receive what they are entitled to.

WARN—WORKER ADJUSTMENT AND RETRAINING NOTIFICATION OF 1988

This law makes it mandatory for an employer who is going to have a "massive layoff" or close a facility to give employees a 60-day notice of its intent if the employer's action involves more than 50 people. The intent is to give affected employees time to find other employment to plan for their employment loss.

BFOQ—BONA FIDE OCCUPATIONAL QUALIFICATION

This makes it possible for an employer to legally impose requirements based on modified categories. For example, some restaurants have men's (or women's) room attendants. It is lawful to exclude females from employment as attendants in male restrooms. However, the provisions should be scrutinized closely, and every job exclusion must be thoroughly documented and based on fact.

COBRA—CONSOLIDATED OMNIBUS BUDGET RECONCILIATION ACT

This act requires most employers with 20 or more employees (except churches and the federal government) to extend health care coverage to terminated employees. The act covers retirees and their spouses, widowed or divorced spouses, dependent children of current or former employees, and employees who voluntarily or involuntarily quit (except those terminated for "gross misconduct"). Normal group coverage is extended for 18 months at the expense of the terminating employee and at no more than 102% of premium costs. It is a good practice to offer COBRA on the last day of employment to make sure you are complying with this act.

EEOC—EQUAL EMPLOYMENT OPPORTUNITY COMMISSION

This agency was created in 1964 with the passage of the Civil Rights Act. The EEOC is granted the authority to investigate claims of discrimination regarding vocational rehabilitation, equal pay, pregnancy discrimination, civil rights, the ADA, and the ADEA. If a claim is filed against an employer, this agency will send the employer a charge with the alleged violation and require the employer to respond to a number of questions so it can determine if an act of discrimination has taken place.

FLSA—FAIR LABOR STANDARDS ACT

This act regulates a minimum wage(s) and overtime, and addresses the use of child labor. It also provides definitions for exempt and nonexempt employees:

Exempt—Those employees classified as executive, administrative, professional, or outside sales are "exempt" from the overtime provisions of the act. Employers do not have to pay them overtime (but can choose to do so in some cases).

Nonexempt/Hourly—All others who must be paid overtime.

IRCA—IMMIGRATION AND REFORM CONTROL ACT

This act, originally passed in 1986, provides penalties to those employers who knowingly hire illegal aliens. The act makes it illegal to discriminate in hiring or terminating on the basis of citizenship or national origin. It also requires the completion of I-9 forms (proof of citizenship or right to work) within 72 hours of hire. Proof of identity (i.e., a birth certificate, driver's license, a Social Security card, or immigration papers) must be supplied, and more than one item is required to prove legal working rights.

FMLA—FAMILY MEDICAL LEAVE ACT OF 1993

This act requires employers with 50 or more employees to provide up to 12 weeks of family leave (without pay). The employee must be returned to the same position or one of equivalent status and pay. To be eligible, an employee must have worked at least 12 months and 1250 hours in the year preceding the request for leave. A total of 12 weeks is allowed during any 12-month period for: (1) the birth, adoption, or foster-care placement of a child, (2) to care for a spouse, parent, or child with a serious health condition, and (3) a serious employee health condition. A person taking the leave should give a 30-day notice if possible, and upon return must be given the same job or one of equivalent status and pay. The leave can be taken in intermittent blocks.

SEXUAL HARASSMENT

All employees must be provided with a work environment free from unwanted or unwelcome conduct. Harassment can be male to female, female to male, or same sex (e.g. male to male). Generally, there are two types of harassment: *quid pro quo* and *hostile environment*. Quid pro quo harassment occurs when a person wants "something for something," such as sex for a promotion. A hostile environment is created when the harassing activity (e.g., continually asking for a date) creates an intolerable working environment. (See *Preventing Sexual Harassment*, HRD Press, 1999.)

EMPLOYMENT AT WILL

This is a doctrine stating that employment is at the will of the employer. Its basic premise is that either the employer or the employee can terminate the employment relationship at any time and for any or no reason or cause. A word of caution: Even at-will employees are modified by antidiscrimination laws such as ADA and ADEA. (See *Documenting Employee Performance*, HRD Press, 1998.)

OSHA-OCCUPATIONAL HEALTH AND SAFETY ACT OF 1970

This act was passed to ensure a safe working environment for all employees. It requires all employers with more than one employee to police working conditions for compliance with mandated safety standards. It is not at all uncommon for OSHA agents to visit a work site unannounced to observe safety practices for compliance. Those found negligent are subject to fines and/or penalities.

NLRB—NATIONAL LABOR RELATIONS BOARD

This board exists to protect the rights of employees who desire to join a union. It also protects an employee's rights *not* to join a union. Where a question of representation exists, the board will conduct an election if 30% of the employees have signed a card requesting union representation.

OFCCP—OFFICE OF FEDERAL CONTRACT COMPLIANCE PROGRAMS

Created by executive order in the 1960s, this agency monitors the affirmative action efforts of businesses with government contracts. Any employer doing business with the U.S. government who has 50 or more employers and $50,000 in sales is required to have an affirmative action plan.

A.A.P.—AFFIRMATIVE ACTION PLAN

A document that measures progress toward the utilization of minorities and females, as defined by local and in some cases national availability (labor market) rates. Where there is under-utilization, *affirmative action* is taken to remedy the situation. Affirmative action can be through recruitment or promotion.

IMPORTANCE OF COMPLIANCE

I have discussed some of the more common laws and regulations affecting managers and their organizations. You must become familiar with them to avoid placing the company in a compromised position. In these instances, a little knowledge is not dangerous, it is critical! Always ask yourself, "If I take this action, is there a resultant reaction?" When it comes to the crazy world of employment law, two heads are *always* better than one.

RECOMMENDED ACTIONS

In any questionable employment situation, I recommend that you do the following if you are uncertain about the situation.

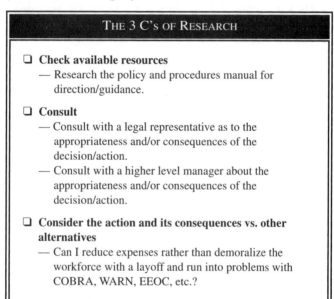

THE 3 C's OF RESEARCH

❑ **Check available resources**
   — Research the policy and procedures manual for direction/guidance.

❑ **Consult**
   — Consult with a legal representative as to the appropriateness and/or consequences of the decision/action.
   — Consult with a higher level manager about the appropriateness and/or consequences of the decision/action.

❑ **Consider the action and its consequences vs. other alternatives**
   — Can I reduce expenses rather than demoralize the workforce with a layoff and run into problems with COBRA, WARN, EEOC, etc.?

The employee relations process begins with a basic understanding of employment law. It continues with an examination of skills and organization practices.

As you read the questions in the next section and research your answers, look closely at the language you find in your policies, procedures, handbooks, application forms, offer letters, etc. There are a few words you will want to eliminate, modify, or add definition to in order to avoid claims based on implied contract rights or covenants of good faith dealings:

- Due process
- Job security
- Just cause
- Guaranteed
- Permanent
- Long term
- Career path
- Secure or secured

These words tend to be interpreted as a commitment to continuing employment. Because you are an *at will* employer, you will want to emphasize this with the appropriate language.

THE EMPLOYMENT PRACTICES AUDIT

Organizational skills and knowledge are needed in a number of differing disciplines in order to be an effective and informed manager. For example, one must be an effective interviewer in order to choose the right person for a specific position. The manager must also have a working knowledge of employment law because of the potential impact of any employee on the business. The manager must also realize that his or her actions can affect the company in that the

manager's representations, including verbal, can be as
binding as any written statement.

The next few pages will cover two critical areas: (1) the
training an organization needs to provide its managers, and
(2) what an organization must do to comply with mandated
laws. Let's look at these in a checklist format:

Recruitment and Hiring

(1) Is there an employee requisition system?

   Yes _____   No _____

Not necessary, but a good idea for expense control and other reasons (see question #2).

(2) Does the requisition define essential functions and take into
consideration the mandates of the ADA?

   Yes _____   No _____

It should to protect against a claim of discrimination. You must outline the duties, especially if they are exclusionary to the disabled or any other protected class.

(3) Are tests part of the hiring process?

   Yes _____   No _____

(4) Are the tests validated?

   Yes _____   No _____

If a test is used, it should be validated. Validation means that it is a quantified predictor
of success on the job and that it is not exclusionary because of race, sex, etc.

(5) Are interviewers trained in the questioning of candidates? Do
they know which questions are legal or illegal?

   Yes _____   No _____

All interview questions should relate only to the specific position and the skills needed
to be successful. The questions must be nondiscriminatory. Questions concerning one's
personal life must be avoided. Also, interviewers must understand the consequences of
their statements. Oral promises, statements, or representations can be binding.

(6) Do you require a pre-employment drug test?

Yes _____   No _____

Pre-employment testing is legally safer than post-employment testing in many states. If you are going to test, this is the time to do it.

(7) Does your application contain questions concerning race, color, religion, sex, national origin, ancestry, age, marital status, child care, pregnancy, or physical impairment?

Yes _____   No _____

Statistics are gathered after hire, not before. Leave these questions off your application. You can ask for these on an addendum to the application. Make sure that you state the requested information is optional and is used only for employment statistics.

(8) Are the employment statistics you gather (after hire) maintained in a file separate from the employee's file?

Yes _____   No _____

These statistics should be maintained in a separate file so that they are not considered in any employment decisions. The person's qualifications are all that matters.

(9) Does the application contain an at-will statement?

Yes _____   No _____

It should, so that no expectation of continued employment is implied.

(10) Do you require an employee to complete an I-9 and submit appropriate documentation within 72 hours?

Yes _____   No _____

This is the law.

(11) Does every employee hired after November 6, 1986 have a completed I-9 (IRCA) form on file?

Yes _____   No _____

Also the law. You can get an I-9 form from the U.S. Department of Justice Immigration and Naturalization Service (form # OMB 1115-0136).

(12) Does your offer letter contain an at-will statement?

Yes _____   No _____

It should as per #9. An employer should standardize the offer letter to make sure it avoids any unintentional contractual statements or commitments.

(13) Are reference checks limited to the human resources department or to a central source that understands the legal ramifications of giving out information that is potentially libelous?

Yes _____   No _____

This is a must; no information should be given that could harm the company.

(14) Are reference checks limited to name, title, and job duties?

Yes _____   No _____

This is recommended. Actionable causes could be the end result if this process is not handled properly.

Organization

(15) Do you have a policy and procedures manual?

Yes _____   No _____

Standardizing your manual will help to prevent miscommunication and unintentional commitments.

(16) Does it contain a disclaimer?

Yes _____   No _____

A disclaimer basically states that the company makes no representation that should be construed as binding, and that contents except for the "at will" employment policy can be changed at any time and for any reason.

(17) Do you have an employee handbook?

Yes _____   No _____

Standardizing your handbook will help to control miscommunication and unintentional commitments. A receipt signed by the employee is encouraged to prove its dissemination and the employee's understanding of it. The receipt should contain a repetition of the "at will" employment policy.

(18) Does it have a disclaimer?

Yes _____ No _____

The handbook should contain a disclaimer stating the company reserves the right to modify terms and conditions except the "at will" employment relationship at its discretion without prior notice.

(19) Do you have a sexual harassment prevention policy and is it posted?

Yes _____ No _____

At a minimum, the policy should state the definitions of harassment, the penalties for violation of the policy, reporting mechanisms, and that it will not be tolerated. It should be posted on all bulletin boards.

(20) Do you have job descriptions, and do the descriptions define needed skills and take into consideration ADA specifics?

Yes _____ No _____

Be accurate; make sure the skills and essential functions necessary for each position are spelled out and that they don't exclude those who are physically or mentally impaired. See the job description format in Appendix I.

(21) Are employment records kept locked and secured?

Yes _____ No _____

Keep all records locked for the protection of each individual's right to privacy.

(22) Are medical records kept separate from personnel records?

Yes _____ No _____

Medical records must be kept separate as described in ADA guidelines.

(23) Do you post the following federal notices? Minimum Wage; Employee Polygraph Protection Act; Equal Employment Opportunity Is the Law; Your Rights under the FMLA, OSHA?

Yes _____ No _____

Obtain these and other posters from the local Department of Labor. Some states have other requirements; check for those, too. And if you are a federal contractor, you will need to post Notice to all Employees and Notice to Employees Working on Federal Contracts.

(24) Is a substance abuse policy posted?

Yes _____ No _____

The policy should be posted and contain language stating that any substance abuse (e.g., drugs, alcohol, etc.), its manufacture, dispensing, possession, or distribution will not be tolerated. It is a good practice to offer rehabilitation to those serious about "kicking" their habit.

(25) Do you post notices relating to equal employment opportunity laws?

Yes _____ No _____

They should contain reference to the ADA, Equal Pay Act, the Equal Employment Opportunity Act, and the ADEA.

(26) If you require pre-employment drug screening, do you state this in your offer letter?

Yes _____ No _____

You should state that any employment offer is contingent on successfully passing a drug screen.

(27) Does the company review its advertisements for discriminatory statements?

Yes _____ No _____

Ads should avoid mentions of race, color, religion, sex, age, national origin, ancestry, or physical or mental disability. Some states require that there be no mention of sexual orientation.

(28) Do managers know and apply the company's overtime rules?

Yes _____ No _____

Make sure managers do not let people work without paying them overtime. Let them know that "side deals" with employees (It's ok with me.) are unacceptable.

(29) If the company searches lockers, purses, etc., is a policy posted to this effect?

Yes _____   No _____

Prior notification will help protect against an employee's right to privacy. You should state that the company retains the right to search desks, lockers, lunch boxes/bags, purses, tools, cars on company property, etc., whenever it feels such searches are necessary.

(30) Does the company allow its managers to terminate without review?

Yes _____   No _____

This practice will, sooner or later, result in a wrongful termination suit. Always consult before termination.

Record Retention

Company practices regarding the retention of personnel records vary, but a good rule of thumb is to keep everything in an employee's file for a minimum of seven years after termination. Many actionable claims will exhaust their limitations within this time frame. There are two notable exceptions to the seven-year rule: records of medical examinations and environmental monitoring of exposures to hazardous material. In these instances the files should be maintained for the duration of employment *plus* 30 years. However, here is some good advice: **Always consult with an attorney before destroying any employee-related material.**

Conclusion/Recommended Actions

We started this chapter by suggesting an internal review of company practices will help the organization train its managers and help it comply with the array of state and federal regulations that impact a business.

FOCUS ON PREVENTIVE MAINTENANCE.

It is now time to develop a plan based on the answers to the survey questions. For example, if you answered "no" to question #5, "Are managers trained to interview?" you should set as a goal for your company: Get those who need the training in an interview skills program this year. A matrix will help you achieve your mission:

To Do	Who	When
Interview training	(Name)	July 10
Post notices		
Update job descriptions		
Maintain and store files		
Ensure privacy of medical records		

The idea is to focus on the gap, decide who needs the training or has the responsibility for corrective action, and set a date for completion.

Words of Wisdom

Earlier in this section, I listed a number of words that should be clarified or defined. I recommend that you eliminate some from your working vocabulary and clarify what you mean by others before you use them.

Words to Eliminate

Court rulings indicate that some words imply a contract of continuing employment. I recommend that you do not use them. If you find them in policy and procedure manuals, handbooks, offer letters, etc., eliminate them completely. Here's a list:

Job security	In today's business world, there is no such thing. Remember that you are an *at will* employer.
Guaranteed	Very little is guaranteed. It is best to avoid this word.
Permanent	Replace this word with *regular*, as in "regular employee" instead of permanent employee.
Long term	Replace with "employment is for no specified period of time."
Career path	Replace with "eligible for progression."
Secure	Nothing is secure where there is an at-will relationship.

A Few Definitions

Due Process

Due process is defined as procedural fairness. The employee must have an opportunity to present his or her side of the story. For example, due process is usually a part of the discipline procedure. The discipline procedure consists of a number of steps and reviews that precede discharge. Employees under due process are allowed to defend themselves at each step. The company must follow the rules as it has created them.

Just Cause

This phrase is associated with the process of termination for "just cause." C. Daugherty has defined it in the arbitration process as:

- A forewarning of the consequences for inappropriate conduct

- Rules found to be reasonably related to the orderly, efficient, safe operation of the business

- The company's efforts to discover if the employee did, in fact, violate or disobey a rule

- An investigation process conducted fairly and objectively

- Substantial proof provided

- Application of rules without discrimination

- Discipline relates to the seriousness of the violation

While it is always advisable to give employees due process and to ensure that you have good cause for termination, you should never promise employees that they will have these rights. If you do, a court can second-guess your actions to decide whether you lived up to your promises. Promising due processing or the need for just cause is the opposite of an at-will employment relationship.

Appendix I

SAMPLE POLICY STATEMENTS AND PROCEDURES

DISCLAIMER

A disclaimer statement should be included in all policy and procedure manuals and employee handbooks. The following material is presented as models only to demonstrate that something similar is needed. It is important that the company's attorney review every disclaimer statement, offer letter, etc., and make necessary changes to comply with state and federal law.

Addendum

Employment "At Will"

Our company believes in and adheres to the doctrine of employment at will, unless or except as modified by applicable law. Provision of this (manual/handbook) should not be interpreted as a promise of continued employment, a guarantee of due process, or a commitment to existing terms or conditions of employment. The company and its employees have the right to terminate the employment relationship, with or without cause, at any time and for any or no reason.

Specific Disclaimers

Progressive discipline is not required or appropriate in every situation. Management retains discretion to discipline and discharge without progressive discipline and with or without cause.

Supervisory statements, facility practices, offers of employment, and written statements are not contractual or enforceable in nature. No Company representative other than the President has any authority to enter into any agreement for any period of time or to make any commitments or promises regarding any benefit or terms and conditions of employment. Any such commitment by the Company must be in writing.

Current compensation and benefit levels and terms are not a contract. Pay and benefit rates and systems are not guaranteed, and may be revised at any time. Vesting statements contained in the retirement plans do not imply a restriction on the right to terminate employment.

SAMPLE OFFER LETTER

Look closely at the following offer letter for employment. It includes several critical concepts:

1. It states the salary offer in monthly terms so as not to imply any employment duration
2. It states that drug screening is a condition of employment.
3. It is ADA-neutral.
5. It contains an *at will* statement to reinforce and define the employment relationship.
5. No language in the letter implies a specific employment duration

Dear Mr. Smith:

I am very happy to extend an offer of employment to you to become our Senior Accountant.

Your starting salary will be at a rate of $4,200 a month and we would like you to begin on March 15. As we discussed in the interview, we will pay your moving expenses per the attached policy. In addition, and as discussed in our interview, you must successfully pass a pre-employment drug screen as a condition of employment. I have arranged for your drug screen at (address). As soon as we have the results, we will contact you to confirm employment if you successfully pass the screen. XYZ is an At Will employer and you or the company can discontinue the employment relationship at any time and for any or no reason.

We look forward to your contributions.

Sincerely,

(Manager)

SAMPLE OPEN DOOR POLICY

It is the intent of XYZ Company to provide a working environment where each employee is free to seek answers to any issues without boundaries. The only way to make this a reality is by practicing an open door policy. Simply stated, all employees are encouraged to see any member of management at any time to seek answers to any questions or to discuss any work-related issue of concern. Managers are charged with the responsibility to be available and to provide feedback within 72 hours of the consultation with the employee. We actively encourage you to use this system and trust that it will bring about early resolution to issues, problems, or concerns.

JOB DESCRIPTION FORMAT
ADA REQUIREMENTS

Most job descriptions are divided into sections. Generally these include an introductory section about the *Organization*, a segment referred to as *Nature and Scope*, and another called *Essential Job Functions*. It is in this last section that you document the duties of the job keeping in mind the requirements of the ADA. You must be factual, accurate, and quantifiable where necessary. If you cannot justify the job requirement; do not list it as a job requirement. Let's look at a sample form:

Environmental Conditions

Describe the environmental conditions and frequency for the items listed below. Frequency is defined as (1) Rarely—Up to 15% of shift, (2) Occasional—Over 16% and up to 40% of shift, (3) Frequent—41% to 70% of shift, (4) Continuous—Over 70% of shift.

Hot environment _____

Cold environment _____

Changing temperatures _____

Humidity _____

Noise levels _____

Physical Requirements:
Write % next to description

Ability to stand _____	Ability to crawl _____
Ability to walk _____	Ability to reach _____
Ability to sit _____	Ability to handle _____
Ability to stoop _____	Ability to finger _____
Ability to kneel_____	Ability to feel _____
Ability to crouch _____	Ability to speak _____
Ability to hear _____	Ability to lift (X) lbs. _____

Ability to carry (X) pounds _____
Ability to push (X) lbs. _____
Ability to pull (X) pounds _____
Ability to ascend (X) ft. _____
Repetitive motion _____
Eye/Hand coordination _____

Visual Requirements:
Write % next to the statement

Describe the necessary visual requirements _____
Ability to see clearly at 20 feet or more _____
Ability to see at 20 inches or less _____
Ability to judge distance and space
   relationships accurately _____
Ability to see peripherally _____
Ability to adjust vision to bring objects into focus _____
Ability to distinguish and identify different colors _____

Physical Context/Work Environment

This position is primarily:

_____   Sedentary work, lifting a maximum of 10 lbs.;
         walking/standing occasionally

_____ Light work, frequent lifting of up to 10 lbs; frequent standing/walking

_____ Medium work, frequent lifting/carrying of objects up to 25 lbs.

_____ Heavy work, frequent lifting/carrying objects of 50 lbs. or more.

SAMPLE COMPLAINT PROCEDURE

Any employee who has a complaint will have an opportunity to have the complaint heard and will receive an answer. Our procedure is as follows:

1. Take your complaint to your supervisor. This individual will investigate the complaint and respond to it within 72 hours. If you are not satisfied with the decision, you may take it to Step Two.

2. Take your complaint to your supervisor's supervisor. This individual will look at the previous decision and the rationale for the decision, investigate it further if needed, and respond within 72 hours. If you are not satisfied with the decision, you may take it to Step Three.

3. Take the complaint to the human resources department. They will look at the previous decisions and their rationale, investigate it further if needed, and review their decision with the President. The human resources department, with the agreement of the President, will render a binding decision.

4. The company reserves the right to deviate from these procedures. Failure to comply with these procedures shall not invalidate any company action. The foregoing does not affect the company's policy of at-will employment.

Appendix II

WHERE TO FIND COMPLIANCE FORMS AND INFORMATION

Let's hope this Pocket Guide has presented information helpful to your company or organization. We advise you to contact the following government agencies for forms, notices, and other compliance information.

- **I-9s**
  Contact the nearest U.S. Department of Justice, Immigration and Naturalization Services (INS) office. Request form OMB# 1115-0136.

- **Equal Employment Opportunity Is the Law (posters)**
  Contact the nearest office of the EEOC or write to:
  Equal Employment Opportunity Commission
  2401 E Street NW
  Washington, DC 20506

- **Federal notices, Job Safety and Health Protection, Employee Polygraph Protection Act**
  Contact the nearest office of the U.S. Department of Labor, Employment Standards Administration.

INDEX

ABOUT THE AUTHOR

Terry Fitzwater is managing partner of FLC Leadership Consulting. His firm specializes in employee relations and organization development. Prior to consulting he spent over 17 years as a human resource executive with a Fortune 100 company. He is a frequent speaker and trainer on various employee relations topics and an adjunct faculty member for a local university instructing management classes. For further information on discipline and documantation, as well as other topics, you can contact Mr. Fitzwater at (916) 791-0692; E-mail, www.tfitzh2o@quiknet.com.